TIME FOR KIDS READERS

AT ARLINGTON

by Justine Ciovacco

Harcourt

Orlando Austin Chicago New York Toronto London San Diego

Visit *The Learning Site!*
www.harcourtschool.com

On a Virginia hillside by the Potomac River and overlooking Washington, D.C., a United States Army officer is being buried. More than 260,000 gravesites and memorials stretch out around the officer's new burial plot. Arlington National Cemetery has more than 20 funerals a day, but the officer's burial is still an important event.

His casket, draped with a U.S. flag, enters the cemetery on a black carriage pulled by horses. The horses climb over Memorial Bridge and stop by the crowd of family, friends, and uniformed soldiers who have gathered to honor the officer for his commitment to his country.

One of six Arlington chaplains, or ministers, conducts a service, mentioning the officer's accomplishments. At the end of the ceremony, a group of soldiers aims its rifles into the air, giving a three-volley salute. Finally, as a bugler sounds "Taps," soldiers lift the flag from the casket, fold it into a triangle, and hand it to the cemetery's superintendent. He gives it to the officer's family.

Being part of Arlington's funerals is a great honor for the soldiers who volunteer to help. "Every team that goes out, its members are trying to make that job the best they have ever done," says Charles Sowles, the leader of the Third U.S. Infantry, which takes part in Arlington's ceremonies.

In the background of this daily scene stands a nineteenth-century mansion called Arlington House. Without this historic building, there may never have been an Arlington National Cemetery.

It is tradition for three of the horses that pull the carriage to be without riders.

TFK DID YOU KNOW

Arlington Firsts and Facts

- First military serviceperson buried: Private William Henry Christman, Sixty-Seventh Pennsylvania Infantry, buried May 13, 1864.
- First to have family present at burial: Private William H. McKinney, Seventeenth Pennsylvania Cavalry, buried late May 13, 1864.
- Digger of first graves: James Parks, a former Arlington House slave. He is the only person buried at Arlington who was born on the property.
- Almost 3,800 former slaves who were living in Freedman's Village at Arlington are buried there. "Citizen" or "civilian" is written on their headstones.

George Washington and his family, including young George Washington Parke Custis

The story of the cemetery started with George Washington Parke Custis. Custis's father, John Parke Custis, was the stepson of George Washington. When John Parke Custis died in 1781, his mother, Martha Washington, invited his young son and daughter to live at Mount Vernon, the Washingtons' Virginia estate.

George Washington welcomed the children as if they were his own. Custis was only three when he began living with his grandparents. Washington soon taught him everything from how to farm to the secrets of politics. He also gave Custis first-hand accounts of the Revolutionary War and America's struggle for independence from Britain. Because of Washington's kindness and intelligence, Custis admired and respected the former President.

When George Washington died in 1799, Custis decided to create a memorial in his honor. The memorial was to be a mansion built on a large family estate, a 1,100-acre spread of land that Custis had inherited from his father. Custis wanted to name the site Mount Washington, but he changed his mind. Instead, he chose for the memorial the name of an earlier Custis family estate in Virginia—Arlington.

To design the mansion honoring Washington, Custis picked George Hadfield, an English architect who helped construct the U.S. Capitol. Custis wanted the building to be grand and elegant, with touches of Greek architecture. When the north wing was completed in 1802, Custis moved in. He brought with him a lot of George Washington heirlooms. His treasures included everything from portraits of his grandfather to Washington's personal papers, clothes, and even the tent that the former general had used at Yorktown—the battle that ended the Revolutionary War.

Within the next two years, the south wing of Arlington House was completed. The house now consisted of two separate buildings. After Custis married Mary Lee Fitzhugh, he continued to live in the north wing of Arlington House. Mary loved to entertain at the estate and was proud of a large rose garden she had planted beside the house.

A central section of the house—with a formal dining room, sitting room, large hall, and parlor—was finished in 1818. Finally complete, Arlington House stretched 140 feet (43 m) from wing to wing. Eight thick Greek-style columns (5 feet—almost 2 m—in diameter at the base) greeted visitors on the front portico, or columned porch.

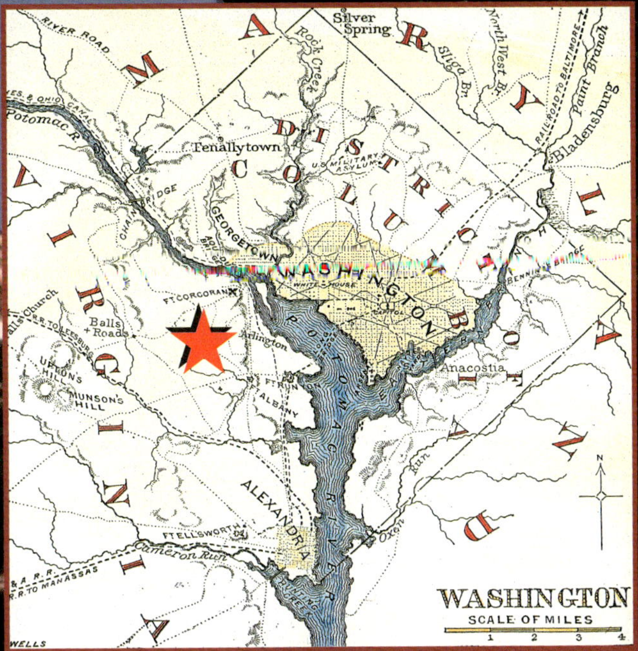

Arlington, Virginia, is across the Potomac River from Washington, D.C.

Construction on Arlington House began in 1802 and took 16 years to complete.

By the time the house was complete, Mary Anna Randolph Custis, the only child of George and Mary, was 10 years old. She grew up to marry a childhood friend Robert E. Lee. Lee was the son of a former Virginia governor and a graduate of the U.S. Military Academy at West Point. The Custis family proudly welcomed their new son-in-law into Arlington House after the couple married on June 30, 1831.

Between 1841 and 1853, Lee often left Arlington House on military business. During this time, his mother-in-law died and was buried on the grounds of Arlington. When his father-in-law died in 1857, Lee rushed home to be with his family.

Custis left Arlington House to Mary Anna. He noted that when she died, her oldest son, George Washington Custis Lee, would own the estate. Robert E. Lee, who had became a major general in the U.S. Army, managed Custis's burial at Arlington as well as much-needed repairs to the mansion.

At the same time, Lee was becoming involved in events that would lead to the Civil War. In April 1861, Virginia joined the Confederacy and seceded from the Union. Lee decided to resign from the U.S. Army so he could fight on the side of Virginia and the South.

Robert E. Lee

"Lee, you have made the greatest mistake of your life," warned an angry General Winfield Scott, Lee's former commander. Because Arlington House was so close to Washington, D.C., the capital of the Union, Lee worried about the safety of his family and home. In May, he wrote to Mary Anna:

"War is inevitable, and there is [no] telling when it will burst around you... You have to move and make arrangements to go to some point of safety which you must select. The Mount Vernon plate and pictures ought to be secured. Keep quiet while you remain, and in your preparations... May God keep and preserve you and have mercy on all our people."

Soon after Lee's family took his advice and left Arlington, federal troops crossed the Potomac River and marched directly to Arlington House. The troops built forts and lived on the property. Lee was upset about losing his family home. Yet, before Arlington was taken over, Lee tried to comfort his wife in another letter.

"They cannot take away the remembrance of the spot, and the memories of those that to us rendered it sacred. That will remain to us as long as life will last, and that we can preserve."

The federal government asked Lee to pay a large amount of money in property taxes to keep the estate. The government took control of Arlington House and its property due to a disputed tax payment. Arlington was put up for public sale on January 11, 1864, and purchased by a tax commissioner for "government use, for war, military, charitable, and educational purposes."

These Union soldiers and their guests were some of the first visitors to Arlington House after it was captured by Union forces in 1861.

Brigadier General Montgomery C. Meigs was put in charge of finding a new use for Arlington. Almost a year before the end of the Civil War, Meigs decreed that the land around Arlington House would be used for a military cemetery. The burial place was named the Arlington National Cemetery.

Under Meigs's orders, one of the first monuments built on the property was for Union soldiers. A stone and cement burial vault 20 feet (6 m) wide by 10 feet (3 m) deep was built in the center of the rose garden. The remains of 1,800 unidentified Union soldiers who had died fighting in Civil War battles were placed in the vault. It is now called the Tomb of the Unknown Dead of the Civil War. Meigs, his wife, his father, and his son were later buried within 100 yards of Arlington House.

Also built on the property was a model community for freed African American slaves. The federal government set up Freedman's Village on December 4, 1863. More than 1,100 former slaves were given land at Arlington. They were allowed to farm the land and make their homes there until they found other places to settle.

Lee and his wife never returned to Arlington. After Lee's death in 1870, his eldest son brought a court case to the Circuit Court of Alexandria (today Arlington) County, Virginia. He claimed that the government had taken the land illegally. George Washington Custis Lee pointed out that, according to his grandfather's will, he was the legal owner. In December 1882, the U.S. Supreme Court returned the property to Custis Lee.

As Freedman's Village (right) grew, it was able to provide schooling for African American children.

Custis Lee knew he could not live at his family estate, among the graves. On March 3, 1883, he sold the property to the U.S. Congress for $150,000 so it could continue to be used as a military graveyard.

Today, almost four million people visit Arlington National Cemetery each year. They come to view not just Arlington House, but also the nearby memorials to some of our nation's greatest heroes.

It is a great honor to be buried at Arlington. That's why some people make special requests to allow special individuals to be buried there. In 1986 Harvard University professor Dr. S. Allen Counter led a movement to have African American explorer Matthew Henson's remains moved from Woodlawn Cemetery in the Bronx, New York, to Arlington.

TFK IT'S A FACT

Famous People Buried at Arlington

- Richard E. Byrd (1888–1957) Navy admiral and explorer of Antarctica
- Medgar Evers (1925–1963) World War II Army veteran and civil rights leader
- John F. Kennedy (1917–1963) U.S. President and World War II Navy veteran (buried with wife, Jacqueline Kennedy Onassis, and two children who died at birth)
- Robert F. Kennedy (1925–1968) World War II Navy veteran, Attorney General, and U.S. senator from New York
- Pierre Charles L'Enfant (1754–1825) Revolutionary War veteran who planned the layout of streets and government buildings in Washington, D.C.
- Joe Louis (1914–1981) Army sergeant and famous boxer
- Lee Marvin (1924–1987) Marine veteran who received the Purple Heart and Academy Award-winning actor
- Audie Murphy (1924–1971) Most decorated soldier of World War II and actor
- Anita Newcomb McGee (1864–1940) Army's first female surgeon
- William Howard Taft (1857–1930) U.S. President and Chief Justice of the Supreme Court

Counter had written a book about Henson, who went on the historic first trek to the North Pole. Henson traveled with naval officer Robert Peary in 1909. The book claimed that Henson was essential to the trip and may have actually been the first person to reach the pole. Though Peary received many honors upon their return, Henson's contributions to the expedition received little credit. Counter's research and dedication paid off in October 1987, when President Ronald Reagan approved Henson for burial in Arlington at a gravesite near Peary's.

Matthew Henson died in 1955. His remains were moved to Arlington 33 years later.

TFK FAST FACTS

Rules for Arlington Burial

To be buried or have ashes stored at Arlington, a person must meet at least one of the following requirements:

- **Died in active military duty.**
- **Retired from active military duty.**
- **Been a veteran who suffered 30 percent or more disability and was honorably discharged from the military before October 1, 1949.**
- **Received one of these military decorations: The Medal of Honor, Distinguished Service Cross, Distinguished Service Medal, Silver Star, or Purple Heart.**
- **Been President of the United States (commander-in-chief of the military).**
- **Been a member of the President's Cabinet, a nationally elected official, or a Supreme Court justice who also served in the military.**
- **Been a husband, wife, or unmarried child under age 21 of one of the above people.**

The President of the United States or Secretary of the Army can give special permission for others to be buried at Arlington. Veterans who were honorably discharged from the military, but do not fit into any of these categories may be inurned (ashes buried after cremation) with their spouses and dependent children.

Workers at the cemetery often place flags near gravesites for Memorial Day.

Arlington is also the site for special services to honor the military. These services often occur on Veterans Day and Memorial Day. Every President since Abraham Lincoln has visited Arlington to honor military heroes and to attend the funerals of friends.

TFK

Memorable Arlington Memorials

- War Correspondents Memorial: A tree offers a living memorial to newspaper reporters who died while reporting on wars.
- Challenger Memorial: This 6-foot-tall marble memorial has a bronze plaque displaying the names of the seven astronauts—including teacher Christa McAuliffe—who died when the space shuttle *Challenger* exploded soon after liftoff on January 28, 1986. The *Challenger* astronauts are buried nearby.
- Tomb of the Unknowns: A marble tomb holds the remains of three unidentified soldiers—one each from World War I, World War II, and the Korean War. They represent all Americans who died in war, and their tomb is guarded by a soldier 24 hours a day.
- Women in Military Service for America: The cemetery's semicircular stone entrance is part of this tribute to the nearly two million women who have served in the United States military since the American Revolution. Four staircases near a reflecting pool lead guests to an education center.

On a visit to Arlington in the early 1960s, President John F. Kennedy stood on the porch at Arlington House and admired the view of the nation's capital in the distance. "I could stay here forever," he said.

When Kennedy died on November 22, 1963, his military background ensured that his burial would be at Arlington. As a Navy lieutenant during World War II, Kennedy was commander of a torpedo boat that was struck by a Japanese destroyer. As his boat broke in half, Kennedy risked his life to save his crew.

On November 25, 1963, a horse-drawn carriage carried President Kennedy's casket across Arlington's Memorial Bridge. Eight soldiers lowered the casket into a hillside grave near Arlington House while 21 guns fired a salute and 51 military planes (one for each state, as well as one for the leader they had lost) flew overhead. The President's widow, Jacqueline Kennedy, and brother, Robert F. Kennedy, lit the Eternal Flame, which continues to burn. It was fitting that this American hero was buried at the place where so many other of our heroes have been laid to rest.

Thousands of people visited the burial site of John F. Kennedy a week after his burial at Arlington.